A TRAVELER'S GUIDE to the SOLAR SYSTEM

BY PATRICIA BARNES-SVARNEY
ILLUSTRATED BY GILBERT FORD

STERLING

New York / London
www.sterlingpublishing.com/kids

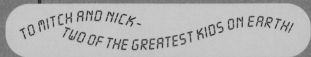

TO MITCH AND NICK — TWO OF THE GREATEST KIDS ON EARTH!

STERLING and the distinctive Sterling logo are registered trademarks of Sterling Publishing Co., Inc.

Library of Congress Cataloging-in-Publication Data

Barnes-Svarney, Patricia I.

Traveler's guide to the solar system / Patricia Barnes-Svarney.

p. cm.

Includes index.

ISBN-13: 978-1-4027-2628-6

ISBN-10: 1-4027-2628-7

1. Solar system—Juvenile literature. 2. Astronomy—Observers' manuals—Juvenile literature.

I. Title.

QB501.3.B372 2008

523.0—dc22   2007012396

10 9 8 7 6 5 4 3 2 1

Published by Sterling Publishing Co., Inc.

387 Park Avenue South, New York, NY 10016

Text copyright © 2008 by Patricia Barnes-Svarney

Illustrations copyright © 2008 by Gilbert Ford

Distributed in Canada by Sterling Publishing

c/o Canadian Manda Group, 165 Dufferin Street

Toronto, Ontario, Canada M6K 3H6

Distributed in the United Kingdom by GMC Distribution Services

Castle Place, 166 High Street, Lewes, East Sussex, England BN7 1XU

Distributed in Australia by Capricorn Link (Australia) Pty. Ltd.

P.O. Box 704, Windsor, NSW 2756, Australia

Sterling ISBN-13: 978-1-4027-2628-6

ISBN-10: 1-4027-2628-7

Designed by Gilbert Ford and Lauren Rille

For information about custom editions, special sales, premium and corporate purchases, please contact Sterling Special Sales Department at 800-805-5489 or specialsales@sterlingpublishing.com.

CONTENTS

WHERE ARE WE GOING?

Some are dusty and dry; others are icy or rocky. Some hide their features from our view with thick clouds; others wear the battle scars from years of space objects hitting their surface. Some are even hot and boiling, while others are so frozen they have looked much the same for billions of years.

SO, WHAT ARE "THEY"? ◄······························

They are nine planets, over 130 moons, and millions of asteroids and comets. And despite their differences, they all have one thing in common. They revolve around our Sun and make up our solar system.

We all know that humans have traveled into space. Twelve astronauts have walked on the Moon and the Space Shuttle astronauts have orbited the Earth.

But unmanned spacecraft have gone much farther. The Venera spacecraft landed on Venus and took the first close-up photographs of the veiled planet's rocky surface. The Magellan craft orbited high above Venus, mapping the surface by taking special radar images through the planet's thick clouds. The Mars Odyssey and Mars Global Surveyor spacecraft orbited high above Mars; the Mars Reconnaissance Orbiter took a low orbit and provided the most vivid images of another planet that we have ever seen; the Vikings and the Pathfinder have landed; and the Opportunity and Spirit rovers have roamed the red planet—and all of them have sent pictures back to Earth. Other spacecraft, such as the Mariners, Pioneers, Voyagers, Galileo, and Cassini, focused on taking photos and allowing scientists to make discoveries about the planets and satellites in the outer solar system. In fact, Pluto and its moon, Charon, are the only planetary

bodies that have not yet been visited, but that will change when the New Horizons satellite arrives at the farthest reaches of our solar system.

By looking at the data and photos that these planetary craft have sent back to Earth, scientists have learned a great deal about our solar system. We can look at the pictures and stretch our imagination, finally understanding what it would be like to walk on the deserts of Mars, plunge through the rings of Saturn, or sunbathe on Mercury.

So how do you use your imagination to travel through space? Most of us know what it's like to stand on a warm sunny beach and feel the sand blow around our feet. Can you feel the small grains strike your legs and cover your toes? No doubt a visit to Mars would "feel" much the same—with one big difference. You would be standing on a sandy desert but it would be freezing.

What about watching storm clouds gather overhead as you run for cover from the rain, thunder, and lightning? You would have the same feelings on Jupiter—but there would be some strange differences. As you watch the huge storm clouds on Jupiter form, you would have nowhere to go, because there is no solid ground on which to run.

We have still only scratched the surface when it comes to learning about the other members of our solar system. There are still mysteries that baffle scientists. But based on our own experiences on Earth, we can guess—and use our imaginations to interpret—what it would feel like to be on other planets and moons.

Now it's time for you to grab a chair and your imagination. Let this book be your guide as you work your way from Mercury to Pluto and all the places in between. It's time to visit some of the wildest, strangest, and most astounding places in our solar system—and we won't stop until we've seen all the sites!

FIRST STOP: MERCURY

Hop on the surface of Mercury and take a look around you. You're standing on the sunlit side of the planet— and it looks as if the Sun is everywhere!

Notice how the Sun covers almost one quarter of the sky. From here it appears over two and a half times larger than the Sun as seen from Earth. Welcome to Mercury, the second smallest planet in our solar system. It is the closest planet to the Sun and, as you'll soon discover, one of the worst places in the solar system to visit.

Why is Mercury so bad? Just look around. There's no wind or breeze; there's no running river water or splashing waves of an ocean. What you will see is that the heat from the Sun bakes everything on the sunlit side of the planet, while everything on the side facing away from the Sun is frozen. On Earth, water vapor and other particles in the air create the blue skies we see. But on Mercury, there's no air or water to scatter the light, so the sky is always black, even in the daytime. As you'll soon discover as you walk around the planet, no plants, animals, or humans could live here without a great deal of protection from the heat, cold, and lack of air.

PLANNING YOUR TIME ◄·····································

If you are looking for a planet that gives you plenty of time to check out the natural wonders, then Mercury is it. The planet spins on its axis about once every 59 Earth days. But be careful when you schedule your itinerary for this planet; there's a trick to defining a Mercury day. Because it takes 59 days to rotate once on the planet's axis and about 88 days to go around the Sun, one "day" on Mercury—or a true sunset to sunset—seems to last two Mercurian years or about 176 Earth days. (To compare, on Earth, the day lasts 24 hours from sunrise to sunrise, and there are about 365 days in a year.) And in fact, because of the strange relation between rotation and revolution, the effect would be a double sunrise. The Sun would rise, dip back to the horizon, and rise again before finally setting for the night.

To see this another way, if you were to stand on Mercury and face the Sun in a specific direction, after about 59 days, you would have made one complete rotation—but you would no longer be facing the Sun. In effect, you would have only been through the daytime and wouldn't have experienced the night. That is because the planet has moved in its orbit as you've been spinning with the planet's axis. It would take three rotations of the planet to return to the same position—or about 176 Earth days—with the planet orbiting the Sun twice in that time. That is why some people say Mercury's true "day" lasts 176 Earth days—plenty of time to get in some sightseeing!

If you plan your trip in terms of Mercury years, be quick. If you stayed on the planet for a while, you'd see that it takes only 88 Earth days for Mercury to make one loop around the Sun. That means if you were 10 years old on Earth, you would be about 41½ Mercury years old. In other words, if you lived on Mercury, you would have already traveled forty-one times around the Sun—instead of only ten times around the Sun on Earth.

ON THE SURFACE

It's time to put on your spacesuit and check out the features of this small planet. Mercury is about 3,030 miles (4,880 kilometers) in diameter; to compare, our Moon is 2,260 miles (3,640 kilometers) in diameter. A quick check of the surface may look familiar. Like the Moon, Mercury has long cracks, single and double craters, bright rays, and even smooth plains.

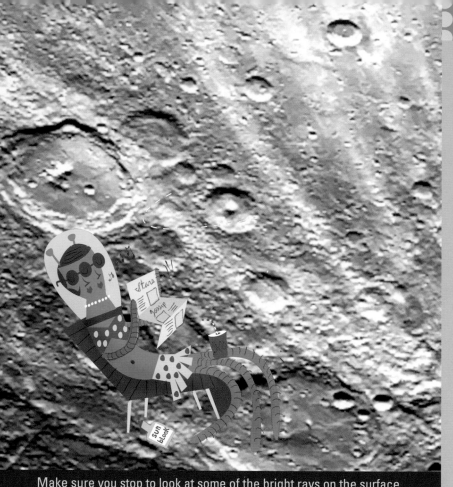

Make sure you stop to look at some of the bright rays on the surface of Mercury, like this field that was formed when a huge space body hit the planet. The material from the space body was thrown into the sky and settled as a field of bright rays.

Be careful when you go for a walk on this planet—the gravity doesn't hug you to the surface as it does on the Earth. In fact, a space traveler who weighs 100 pounds (45.36 kilograms) on Earth will only weigh 38 pounds (17.24 kilograms) on Mercury. But if you want to practice your sports skills while on vacation, you've come to the right place. You could actually whack a golf ball or hit a softball into orbit. And a jump ball in a game of basketball would allow you to leap 10 feet (3 meters) or more in a single bound.

While you're exploring the surface of Mercury, don't forget a stop off at the Caloris Basin, a huge crater measuring 808 miles (1,300 kilometers) across—thought to have been formed by an impact with a meteoroid, asteroid, or comet. Another great spot to visit is on the opposite side of the planet from the Caloris Basin, where the features seem weird—a jumbled mix of hills and cracks everywhere. Scientists think the shock wave from the huge impacting body that formed the Caloris Basin "shook" the pieces of rock and soil on the opposite side of the planet.

You'll also see some deep, long surface cracks on your tour of Mercury. Many of these long cliffs cut through craters, mountains, and other features—some up to hundreds of miles in length and as much as a mile and a half (3 kilometers) high. Where did these cracks originate? Some scientists believe that billions of years ago, when Mercury first formed, the planet was larger. At one time, the relatively immense core of Mercury may have been made of churning liquid metal and rock. Since that time, the planet has cooled and shrunk (and much of the liquid interior has hardened), creating these strange, long cracks and arid landscapes, much like an apple that shrivels and cracks in the Sun as it dries.

HOTTEST OR COLDEST? ◄ ·······························

You should have packed both summer and winter clothing. Mercury holds a major record in the solar system. It has the largest temperature difference—over 1,000 degrees Fahrenheit (537 degrees Celsius) between day and night temperatures. On the side not facing the Sun, you'll notice temperatures dropping to about –274 degrees Fahrenheit (–170 degrees Celsius), or around eight times colder than a refrigerator. On the sunlit side, the temperature would melt lead—and probably us—soaring to 800 degrees Fahrenheit (427 degrees Celsius) or higher. Mercury definitely isn't the right place to enjoy either summer or winter activities.

But Mercury does have one activity that can't be beat. Look into the planet's daytime sky. You could see the stars if the Sun wasn't so bright. So if it's stargazing your after, Mercury is the hot spot of the solar system—but only on the side facing away from the Sun. The lack of a thick layer of air, or atmosphere, makes it easy to see deep into our universe.

INSIDE MERCURY ◄

There's no way you can travel inside Mercury—but that doesn't stop scientists from guessing about the small planet's interior. They believe the planet has layers like an onion. The inner layer is called the core, and is probably made up of the metals iron and nickel with a modest amount of hot liquid rock slowly moving and cooling. Above this are a thin mantle, and finally, the outer layer called the crust, made of solid rock similar to the surface of our Moon.

Our tour of Mercury has shown that the planet has no atmosphere. But it may have had an atmosphere when the solar system first formed. Because the planet is so close to the Sun, the intense heat probably boiled away Mercury's original blanket of air long ago. What's left is an extremely thin layer of atoms blasted off the surface by particles from the Sun. There are very small amounts of potassium, sodium, helium, hydrogen, and even oxygen atoms—but not enough for even tiny bacteria to breathe.

If you're looking for night life—or any life—on Mercury, you probably won't find it. Life as we know it needs air in order to breathe and moderate temperatures. If there is life on Mecury, it's probably very different from what we are used to on Earth.

core

mantle

crust

Mercury

A scientific guess at Mercury's interior

MERCURY FROM EARTH

Don't forget to take one final look back at Mercury as we continue on our tour. This may be your last chance to get a really good look at the small planet.

The view from here is quite different from that back on Earth. Because Mercury is so close to the Sun, few people on Earth have ever seen the planet with the naked eye. And like our Moon, the small planet has phases, which make it harder to see. However, when it is visible, it is one of the brightest objects in the sky.

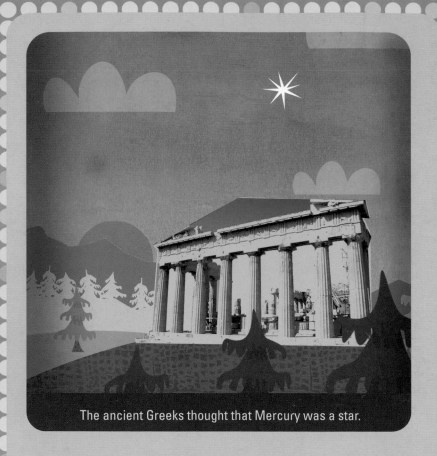

The ancient Greeks thought that Mercury was a star.

There's another reason why you won't often see the planet from Earth. It's only visible about six or seven times a year. It appears as an "evening star" after dusk or "morning star" before sunrise—although it is not really a star. In fact, the ancient Greeks did not realize the difference. They called the planet "Mercury" when they saw it in the evening and "Apollo" when they saw it in the morning.

SECOND STOP: VENUS

This is what Venus will look like once you get past all of the clouds. The bright area near the center has many mountains. The dark areas are smoother.

SECOND STOP: VENUS

Don't bother bringing your umbrella to our next stop, the cloud-covered planet Venus. It will melt! Although Venus is called our "sister" planet, it does not have much in common with the Earth except for its size. Standing on its surface, you can see that it's extremely hot and dry. If you look up, the sky is constantly covered with thick, yellow, sulfuric acid clouds. You may put it on your tour list as another of one of the worst places in the solar system to visit—but it does have some of the most amazing attractions.

IT'S HOT ON VENUS ◀..

Visiting Venus, you'll immediately notice that you have to turn up the air conditioner in your spacesuit—because this planet has the highest surface temperatures of any planet in the solar system. The temperatures can reach around 900 degrees Fahrenheit (482 degrees Celsius)—well above the melting point of lead. Even for travelers seeking warm weather, this may be a bit too much. If you're wondering why Venus is so hot, there is a good explanation. If you had visited the young planet over four billion years ago, you probably would have found vast oceans, much like those on Earth today. But according to modern theories, the blaring heat of the Sun caused the young Venus to rapidly lose its hydrogen atmosphere. The oceans completely evaporated, filling the atmosphere with huge amounts of carbon dioxide. Now the planet's atmosphere is about 96 percent carbon dioxide—or ten thousand times the amount found in the Earth's atmosphere.

Even though only 20 percent of the energy from the Sun is actually able to pierce the clouds and reach the planet,

Venus's thick blanket of carbon dioxide holds the heat tightly to the planet—something that you'll find pretty obvious as you stand on the planet's surface. This is caused by what is called the "greenhouse effect." The thick blanket of carbon dioxide, combined with water vapor from the ancient oceans and sulfuric acid from volcanoes, acts like the glass walls of a greenhouse, holding the stifling heat at the planet's surface. In fact, if there was no greenhouse effect on Venus, you would probably find your visit much more pleasant—as surface temperatures would be similar to the Earth's.

CAN YOU STAND THE PRESSURE?

As with most tour destinations, the weather plays a huge factor when packing your suitcase. When traveling to Venus, an important fact will affect your packing list: The air pressure here is close to ninety times greater than on Earth. Such pressures make it feel similar to diving 3,000 feet (900 meters), or about a half a mile into the Earth's oceans—or as if three full-grown elephants were sitting on top of you! If you landed on the surface of Venus with no protection, you would be crushed immediately. In fact, spacecraft that have landed on our sister planet lasted from only a few minutes to just over an hour—then they were flattened by the immense pressure. That means the only way for you to visit Venus is in a very strong, pressurized spacecraft similar to miniature submarines that dive deep into the Earth's oceans. And because of the heat, our Venus craft would also need a good air conditioner.

HIGHS AND LOWS

Once on Venus, make sure you stop at the two major continent-like highlands that rise over gigantic plains. You may want to grab your best hiking boots. If you're up for a good trek, the highland to the north would be the perfect place to visit. This is Ishtar Terra, an area about the size of

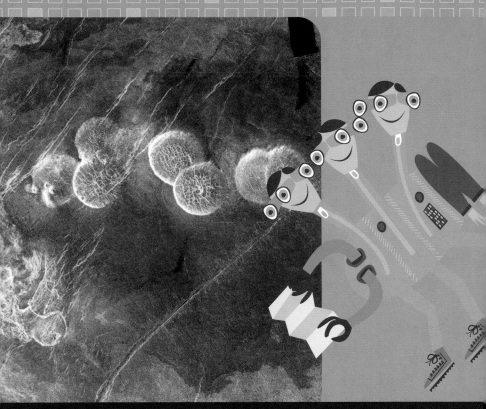

These circular, dome-like hills in the area known as Alpha Regio are just one of Venus's many amazing attractions. It is thought that the hills formed when thick lava erupted from a volcano on a flat plain.

Australia, and home to Venus's highest mountain range, called Maxwell Montes. (This range is also the only feature on the planet named after a male, Scottish scientist James Maxwell; the rest are named after real or mythical females). The peaks in the mountain range are also impressive, some rising more than 6,500 feet (2,000 meters) higher than the Earth's highest mountain, Mount Everest, which measures 29,035 feet (8,850 meters).

The other vast highland you can hike is called Aphrodite Terra—an area about the size of South America and located along the planet's equator. You'll need your strongest hiking boots here, too, as there are several mountain chains and

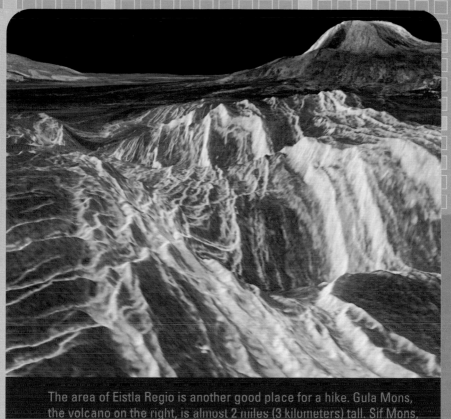

The area of Eistla Regio is another good place for a hike. Gula Mons, the volcano on the right, is almost 2 miles (3 kilometers) tall. Sif Mons, the volcano on the left, is just over 1 mile (1.5 kilometers) tall and measures 186 miles (300 kilometers) across.

lava flows covering the area. In fact about 80 percent of the planet is covered in dried lava fields. But you won't get as worn out here—the mountains are small compared to those in Ishtar Terra.

IT'S IN THE AIR ◀ ·······································

If there was a way to walk on the surface of Venus, it might almost be comfortable—that's because you weigh almost the same as on Earth. For example, if you weigh 100 pounds (45.36 kilograms) on Earth, you'll weigh about 91 pounds (41.27 kilograms) on Venus.

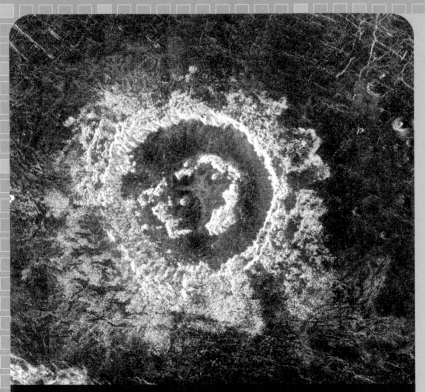

Be sure to check out the craters on Venus, like the Barton crater, named after Clara Barton, founder of the Red Cross. The rings of material surrounding this crater are a good indication that it is an impact crater.

And if you could stand on the surface, you'd notice that the hot, thick atmosphere blocks most of the views. It seems like an overcast day on Earth, but everything has a yellowish tinge. In fact, the yellow color is caused by sulfur particles in the air. But don't take off your spacesuit helmet because you really don't want to breathe in the air. Sulfur gas smells like rotten eggs—and is very poisonous.

Look up at the creamy yellow clouds—and don't forget your sunglasses. It looks as bright as an overcast day on Earth. If you look closely, the clouds seem to be raining. They are made of sulfuric acid and release burning "acid drops." But you still won't need that umbrella. Because of the high heat, the acid drops evaporate before they even reach the ground. Here's a fun Venus activity to try. Pick up a flat stone and drop it. Because of the thick atmosphere, the stone flutters slowly to the ground, like a coin dropping through water on Earth. Next try walking—the real challenge on Venus. Not only is it difficult to walk through the thick atmosphere, but the slightest breeze will push you back. It's like trying to walk through maple syrup.

You'd better stay at the surface for most of this tour. Here, the winds are merely a gentle breeze. If you took any flights into the atmosphere, it would be dangerous—the next cloud level winds move faster than hurricane winds, averaging about 100 miles (160 kilometers) per hour. Even higher in the atmosphere are extreme winds. Here, the clouds move as fast as the jet streams on Earth, or about 220 miles (355 kilometers) per hour. But the prize for the fastest winds goes to the middle cloud layer. These winds can reach close to 450 miles (724 kilometers) per hour—faster than any tornado ever recorded on Earth.

PLANET DAYS ◄···

If you managed to survive on Venus for a while, you'd notice that the planet's year—or how many times the planet races around the Sun—is only 225 Earth days. That means if you were 10 Earth years old, you would be about 16 1/4 Venus years old. But your days on the planet would go slower. One Venus day is equal to 243 Earth days—or 18 days longer than Venus's year. Wouldn't it be nice to have a whole Venus day to read, play, and explore?

Don't get too dizzy as you watch the Venus days go by. Venus rotates retrograde, or spins "backward" when compared to Earth. In other words, the Sun rises in the west and sets in the east—just the opposite of our planet.

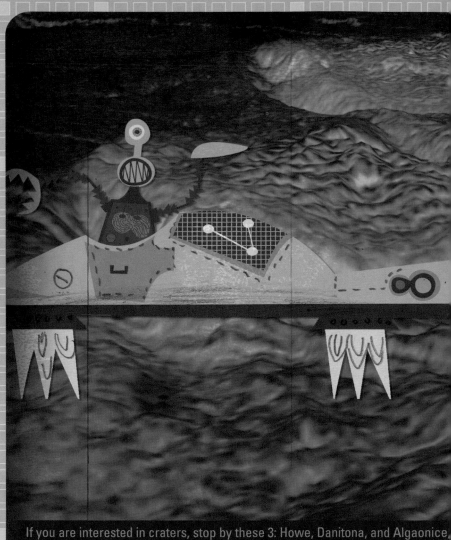

If you are interested in craters, stop by these 3: Howe, Danitona, and Algaonice, shown here in simulated color based on photos taken by the Venera 13 and 14 spacecraft

Would you see life on Venus? It is hard to say. The planet seems too hot for any type of complex life as we know it. The pressure would also be too great to support Earth-like animals, plants, and humans. Could some kind of life have evolved that would not be affected by such harsh conditions? No one knows for sure.

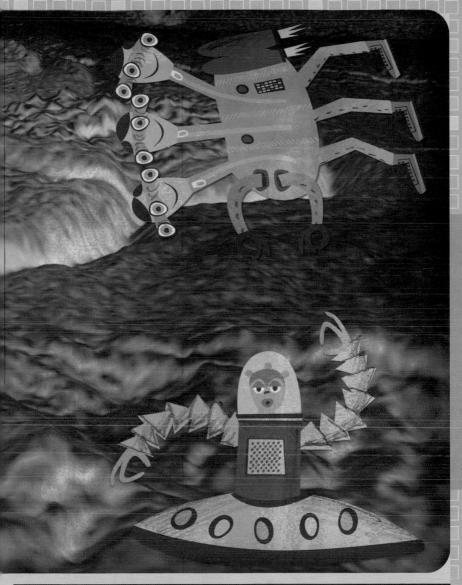

VENUS ROCKS

If you're standing on the surface of Venus, you'll see how the high heat and pressure cause objects in the distance to shimmer, like looking over a blazing campfire on Earth. Through the wavy air, you just might be able to make out rocky crater rims and tall mountains. Most of those tall mountains are actually volcanoes—and if you stayed long enough, you would count more than one thousand scattered across the planet's surface. In fact, the most amazing attractions about Venus are its volcanic lava plains, flows, and domes—all of which cover close to 85 percent of the planet's surface.

Before you leave the planet, be sure to look for craters. You may find that there are relatively few compared to Mercury, Mars, and the Moon. This is because Venus uses its massive volcanic power to regenerate its surface rather often, at least in space terms. In fact, as recently as 500 million years ago, over 80 percent of the planet's surface sank beneath an upwelling of lava that burst through the crust of the planet—like the eruption of one big volcano. The result was a much smoother planetary surface.

VENUS FROM EARTH ◄··

Take a minute and pretend you're back on Earth, looking at Venus. At certain times, Venus is brighter than any planet or star in the Earth's sky (except for the Sun, of course). It is so bright that it can often be seen during the day—and may even cast a shadow at night. And because Venus orbits between the Sun and Earth, it has phases, much like our Moon. When Venus is brightest to an observer on Earth, it is in the crescent phase; when it is in full phase, it is not as bright. (This is the opposite of our Moon, in which a full face is the brightest and the crescent not as bright.) The crescent of Venus is brighter because the planet is closer to the Earth during that phase.

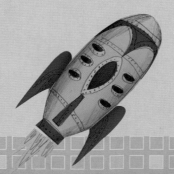

THIRD STOP: MARS

THIRD STOP: MARS

You probably already know that the third planet from the Sun is Earth, but for now, let's move on to Mars—a planet about half the size of Earth.

If you spend some time on Mars, you'll notice that the days are just a little longer than on Earth—around 24 hours and 37 minutes. If you stay long enough on Mars, you'll also notice that the planet has four seasons, much like Earth. But because Mars orbits the Sun in 687 Earth days (or 1.88 Earth years), each season on the planet lasts close to six Earth months. And don't get your hopes up to see fall leaves or springtime growth on the red planet—or even rain or sleet. The seasons on Mars are marked by frost on the rocks, maybe some snows in colder regions, and the strength of planet-wide dust storms.

Take some time to explore the sky on Mars. You won't see this pink daytime sky anywhere else in the solar system.

While on the planet, you'll soon realize that one of its main attractions is its sky. Mars is a planet with pink daytime skies and deep blue sunrises and sunsets. The pink skies are caused by the reflection of iron-rich dust in the air—iron that has turned to "rust," making the particles red. The lack of a thick atmosphere gives the planet its deep blue skies around sunsets and sunrises. Like Mercury, the red planet's dark nighttime sky makes it another great destination for stargazing.

Make sure you bring a good spacesuit for the surface of the planet. The atmosphere is thin and poisonous, made up of almost pure carbon dioxide. And the spacesuit should be pressurized, as the pressures are very low on the red planet.

ICE AT THE POLES

Although it's hard to ski in a spacesuit, there may be a chance to do so. Much like Earth, Mars has two polar ice caps—like two thick, white patches on either end of the red planet. Both of them have strange, swirling designs—the result of layers of dust and ice deposits over time. The planet's northern ice cap is made of water-ice. The southern cap was once thought to be frozen carbon dioxide, or what we call "dry ice." But data from Mars-orbiting spacecraft suggest that it may be made of water-ice, with a thin layer of frozen carbon dioxide on its surface.

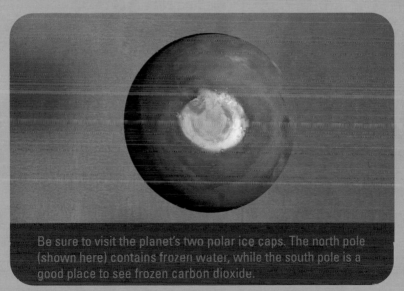

Be sure to visit the planet's two polar ice caps. The north pole (shown here) contains frozen water, while the south pole is a good place to see frozen carbon dioxide.

If you visit Mars for more than one season, you'll want to keep checking out the ice caps. You'll see them change in size, with the caps growing larger in the winter and smaller in the summer. The Martian southern ice cap measures about 250 miles (400 kilometers) across during the southern hemisphere's summer, or when the south pole is pointed toward (and the planet is closest to) the Sun. The northern ice cap stays much larger during its summer, measuring around 621 miles (1,000 kilometers) in diameter. This is because it is colder in the northern hemisphere's summer than in the southern hemisphere's summer—so the ice does not melt as much.

BIG FEATURES ON A SMALL PLANET

This planet truly has some of the "biggest" attractions on our tour. In fact, you may want to pack an extra lunch if you decide to hike some of the Martian volcanoes, as some are many times larger than any on Earth. Whatever you do, be sure to include Olympus Mons on your "must visit" list.

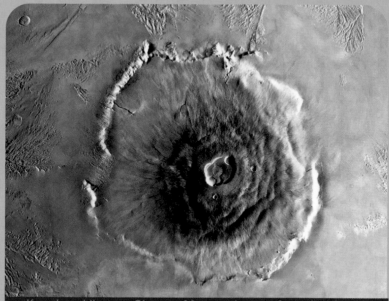

If you're a hiker, put Olympus Mons at the top of your list. As the tallest mountain in the solar system, the view will be well worth the climb. Even if you're not a hiker, check it out anyway. The tall mountain is an impressive sight.

Although it has probably not been active for millions of years, it is the tallest known volcano on Mars and the tallest known volcano in the solar system. Olympus Mons averages about 375 miles (600 kilometers) in diameter and rises about 16 miles (26 kilometers) above the surface. That makes the mountain almost as tall as three Mount Everests, about as wide as the entire Hawaiian Islands chain, and larger than the state of Washington. Strewn across the Martian fields are both big and small chunks of red and black volcanic

You'll want to bring some rope with you to explore Valles Marineris. This 4 mile- (6-kilometer) deep chasm is almost 2,500 miles (4,023 kilometers) long!

rocks. These rocks are the result of ancient eruptions of the many volcanoes that dot the planet.

Your visit to Mars wouldn't be complete without stops to several of the larger canyons and channels on Mars. Make sure you see the largest canyon, Valles Marineris, a deep chasm that would stretch across the entire United States or the Australian continent. It is close to 2,500 miles (4,023 kilometers) long and averages about 4 miles (6.5 kilometers) deep. To compare, the Earth's Grand Canyon is only 1 mile

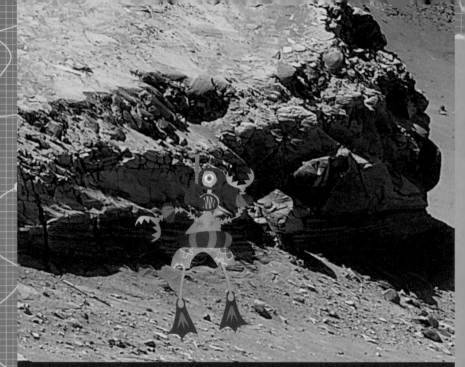

Although scientists believe Mars once had water, they still don't know how or when. Cape Verde is a good place to stop if you want to look for evidence. Here you can see the erosion of the rock where scientists believe the water used to be.

(about 1.5 kilometers) deep. You can also visit many Martian channels similar to rivers back on Earth—but in the case of Mars, there is no water in the channels.

And don't forget to check out some of the biggest Martian craters during your travels. Hellas Planitia (or Hellas Impact Basin) in the southern hemisphere, is the largest crater on the red planet measuring about 1,305 miles (2,100 kilometers) in diameter. Another is the Argyre Basin—a crater about 435 miles (700 kilometers) across.

A NICE DAY ON MARS?

You'll have to plan for all types of weather on Mars. Why? Just look into the sky again. There are water-ice and carbon dioxide clouds, fog, and hazy days—and sometimes even huge storm systems that resemble Earth's hurricanes. As on Earth, these features all form as a result of seasonal temperature changes—in other words, the Martian winter, spring, summer, and fall.

You may want to avoid traveling to Mars during the change of seasons, even though an amazing event occurs—huge dust storms. They can last for months, so if you do go, you'll need some sturdy shelter to protect you. The winds often reach several hundred miles per hour, stirring up the red dust. After eons of time, dust from these storms has settled everywhere, leaving behind some strange attractions—huge sand dunes, thick deposits of dust, and deeply carved canyons and craters.

But you'll have to be extra careful. Often during these storms, tornado-like towers of wind and Martian soil rise 5 miles (8 kilometers) into the sky. These so-called "dust devils" travel at speeds of up to 100 miles (160 kilometers) per hour. You've probably seen a dust devil on Earth. Next time you're in a parking lot or desert on a hot, dry day, notice how the winds pick up dust, leaves, pieces of paper, and dirt, and swirl them around. You are watching a miniature dust devil.

The temperatures on Mars are much colder than those on Earth, so let's hope your spacesuit has a heater. The temperature on the red planet varies from day to night and from season to season. The average temperature on the planet is −67 degrees Fahrenheit (−55 degrees Celsius). The maximum temperature reaches 80 degrees Fahrenheit (27 degrees Celsius), and the minimum temperature gets down to −207 degrees Fahrenheit (−133 degrees Celsius).

But there is great potential for Mars as a holiday spot—in spite of its harsh environment. In fact, many people believe it may be the only planet in the solar system on which we can build a space colony.

What could you expect if you lived in a Martian city? You would always need a special spacesuit to protect you from the cold and lack of breathable air. And you would need protection from solar flares—strong explosions of radiation that come from the Sun's atmosphere and are deadly to people. You would also need strong buildings to keep away from the dust storms. Because the gravity is so low, you would need lead weights in your boots to weigh you down. After all, if you weighed 100 pounds (45.36 kilograms) on Earth, you would only weigh 39 pounds (17.69 kilograms) on Mars. And you would need a place to grow food—because a supply ship would take between six and eight months to get from Earth to Mars.

TWO TINY MOONS

Let's spend a quiet evening on Mars. As you gaze into the nighttime sky, you may see a blue-white crescent close to the horizon. It is the Earth, but it seems no larger than Jupiter does from our planet.

As you watch a little longer, a potato-shaped object appears on the horizon. It's Phobos, a Martian moon that travels around the planet in only 7 hours and 39 minutes. A second moon, Deimos, also has an elongated shape, but it moves slower around Mars. It takes about 30 hours—6 hours longer than the Martian day. But you'll notice a strange occurrence. Because Phobos passes Deimos in the Martian nighttime sky and is orbiting faster than the planet's rotation, it appears to go in the opposite direction when compared to other planets and stars—appearing to travel from west to east

Besides excellent stargazing—because of the planet's thin atmosphere—these moons are the two main attractions in the Martian nighttime sky. Both are small. Phobos measures an average of 15 miles (24 kilometers) in diameter. In fact, if you took a side trip to either moon, you'd be in for a big

Don't leave Phobos without visiting Stickney, a crater over 6 miles (9.5 kilometers) wide. The boulders on the edge of the crater, some of which are over 160 feet (50 meters) wide, are thought to be ejected material from the impact that formed Stickney.

surprise. A 100-pound (45.36 kilograms) person on Earth would weigh only 0.61 ounces (17.29 grams) on Phobos. Deimos is even smaller, measuring an average of 9 miles (15 kilometers) in diameter; a 100-pound (45.36 kilogram) person would weigh only 0.34 ounces (9.64 grams) there. In other words, both moons are so tiny that if you ran as fast as possible, you could launch yourself into space.

You'll no doubt notice something else odd about the moons. Phobos and Deimos always point the same faces towards the planet—just like one side of our own Moon always faces the Earth. If you brought your binoculars, you would see that the surface of Phobos is covered with tiny grooves, small craters, and dust. It does have one huge feature—the crater Stickney, a hole so large it covers almost one third of the moon. Take a look at Deimos, too. It is also covered with craters, grooves, and dust, but it is much smoother than Phobos.

Where did these small moons originate? There has been a great deal of debate about this question, but most scientists believe the two moons formed when the solar system was very young. As the small chunks wandered the solar system, they were snared by the red planet's gravitational pull and are now in orbit around Mars.

If you were to stay on Mars long enough—say, tens of millions of years—you might be in for a big surprise. It is thought that Phobos, the largest of the Martian moons, will one day break up and crash into the red planet—no doubt creating a long line of huge craters on the planet's surface. Phobos' sibling moon, Deimos, will have a different fate—it will eventually escape the pull of the planet's gravity and stop orbiting Mars.

WHAT ELSE YOU'LL FIND OR WON'T FIND

Will you run into life on the red planet or its moons? Many craft have been to the planet, including those that have landed on the surface. But data from the craft have not shown any true signs of life. With more spacecrafts to come, scientists hope to one day find evidence of even the smallest bacteria on the red planet—proof that life exists on another planet in our solar system. And who knows? Maybe one day, if humans walk on the red planet, they may find some evidence of life from the past, like fossils, or even find living organisms that we can't detect using spacecraft.

Let's think back to Earth for a moment. On our planet, river channels carry tons of water over certain paths, flow over the land, and cut into the rock and soil. We can't miss the same thing on Mars. The long winding channels, some larger than the Earth's Amazon Basin in South America, cut into the planet. But you'll definitely notice that something is missing. Where is the Martian water that carved the channels? As you explore the planet, you'll notice that there is a small amount of water trapped in the permanently frozen ground, the ice caps, the thin wispy clouds, and ground frost on cold Martian mornings. But unlike what you're used to on Earth, there is no liquid water to explain the huge channels that crisscross the planet.

So how did water flow on Mars create some of these features? No one really knows. One theory is that Mars was once much warmer and wetter, with a thicker atmosphere, and contained lakes or oceans, rivers, and even rain. Another theory is that Mars was always cold, but water trapped as underground ice periodically melted. It is thought that heating from inside the planet caused ground ice to melt and water to gush onto the surface.

When it comes to the red planet, what happened to the water is the greatest question of all. Scientists have several theories, but none has yet been confirmed. One day we hope to know the answer.

DO YOU BELIEVE IN MARTIANS?

Think back to Earth again. Have you ever seen Mars through a telescope? If you have, you've probably seen strange dark blobs and lines on the surface of the planet. These shapes appear because of the way light reflects off craters, deep canyons, long curved channels, and other Martian features we've seen on our tour.

In the early 1900s, many astronomers looked through their telescopes and saw these shapes on the planet. They thought the patterns were evidence of living beings on Mars. Although there are science fiction stories written about Mars and Martians, we now know that no such beings exist. If there is, or ever was, some type of life on the planet, it would be too small to be detected by our current spacecraft. But future expeditions to the red planet are likely to focus on just this—proving that there's life in the solar system beyond Earth.

FOURTH STOP: ASTEROIDS

FOURTH STOP: ASTEROIDS

D o you like rocks? How about rocks as big as a house? Or as large as the Sears Tower in Chicago? Or how about a rock almost as large as the state of Texas? There are such rocks in the solar system and they are called asteroids. In fact, a trip through the solar system wouldn't be complete without stopping at the "asteroid belt," a collection of boulders and rocks that lies just past the orbit of Mars and before the gas giant Jupiter.

If you visit the asteroid belt, hundreds of thousands of asteroids, from boulder-sized to huge worlds nearly 600 miles (965 kilometers) across, will be in your view. Notice, too, that the majority of these rocks orbit the Sun and none seems to have an atmosphere. If you look closely, you can see that some of the asteroids even have companion moons revolving

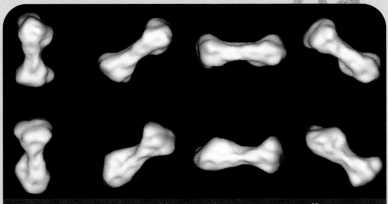

While you're in the asteroid belt, make sure you stop off at Kleopatra. Scientists believe that the dog bone–shaped asteroid is made up of material left over from a violent cosmic collision.

around them, similar to how the Moon revolves around the Earth. One such asteroid is 35-mile-wide (56 kilometers) Ida with its moon Dactyl, a tiny body just over a half mile wide(1 kilometer).

ROUGH ROCKS ◄ ....

Look around the asteroid belt. Needless to say, these rocky bodies are very different from the rocks in your backyard or other colorful rocks and minerals found on Earth. Because most asteroids are small, they don't have enough gravity to pull them into a round form. You can easily spot this as you view the asteroids. The majority of asteroids have odd shapes—including angular, boxy, and even potato- and peanut-shaped ones. While you're here, don't forget to take a side trip to one of the oddest-looking known asteroids. It is called Kleopatra—an asteroid that looks like a 137-mile-long (220 kilometers) dog bone.

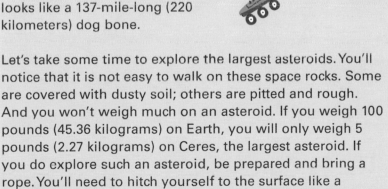

a Fabulous New asteroid belt!

Let's take some time to explore the largest asteroids. You'll notice that it is not easy to walk on these space rocks. Some are covered with dusty soil; others are pitted and rough. And you won't weigh much on an asteroid. If you weigh 100 pounds (45.36 kilograms) on Earth, you will only weigh 5 pounds (2.27 kilograms) on Ceres, the largest asteroid. If you do explore such an asteroid, be prepared and bring a rope. You'll need to hitch yourself to the surface like a mountain climber so you won't float away into space.

If you look carefully at some asteroid surfaces, you will notice various shades of dark and light. The brighter asteroids are thought to contain such metals as iron and nickel. The darker ones are probably made of carbon materials. How do scientists know the composition of these faraway space rocks? There have been several spacecraft flybys of asteroids, and chunks of space rock called meteorites have fallen to the Earth and been analyzed. Most of these space rocks probably came from the asteroid belt (and others may have come from the Moon and Mars).

Did you notice that not all asteroids stay within the asteroid belt? Sometimes these rocks are pulled by the gravity of the planets, including Mars, Jupiter, and even the Earth. Or one asteroid can collide with another in the asteroid belt, causing one or both to fly off into strange orbits. Either way, such

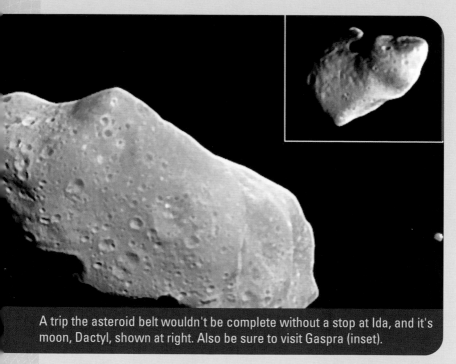

A trip the asteroid belt wouldn't be complete without a stop at Ida, and it's moon, Dactyl, shown at right. Also be sure to visit Gaspra (inset).

wandering asteroids can fall into weird orbits, coming close to planets such as Mars or Jupiter. Some wayward asteroids have been knocked even farther from the asteroid belt— coming close to the Earth as they orbit around the Sun.

By now you may notice that the asteroids are much smaller than any of the planets you've visited so far. And you may wonder how we found out about these small objects in space. In the late 1700s, astronomers thought there might be a planet between the orbits of Mars and Jupiter. In 1801, as Italian astronomer Giuseppe Piazzi was making a star catalog, he noticed a starlike point in his telescope. The next night, the point of light had moved—not like a star, but like a planet. Piazzi had discovered the first asteroid, a 580-mile-diameter (933 kilometers) asteroid he named Ceres, after the Sicilian goddess of grain. Since that time, astronomers have classified more than 100,000 asteroids, with thousands more discovered every year.

Be sure to keep an eye out for comets, such as the comet NEAT, pictured here. In this viewing, you can clearly make out both the head and tail of the comet.

As we glance around the asteroid belt, you'll notice that the rocks look a great deal like other smaller bodies in the solar system called comets. Cousins of the asteroids, comets are a mixture of ices (both water and frozen gases) and dust, and most of them swing in large orbits around the Sun.

What would it be like to visit a comet? Most comets would look like piles of rough rock and ice. And because the tail is made of dust and gas, you could easily pass through it without even noticing. Of course, you would have to watch out for small debris—most of these particles race through the tail at the speed of a bullet.

You've probably seen pictures of comets as they travel around the Sun, and you may have even seen one in the

If you plan your trip at the right time, you may be able to spot Halley's comet. This comet, which appears every 76 years, has been spotted since 240 BC.

nighttime sky back on Earth. One of the main attractions is the comet's long tail. As it gets close to the Sun, the dust and gases boil off from the Sun's heat. Some comets appear once, then disappear into the solar system, never to return; others regularly return to the inner solar system. One such object is Comet Halley—a regular visitor to our nighttime skies every 76 years. Its last appearance was in 1986; it should appear again in 2061.

Like asteroids, comets have struck the Earth in the distant past. And they have also slammed into other planets. One of the most exciting was the Shoemaker-Levy 9 comet. If you had been on a tour of Jupiter in July of 1994, you might have seen 21 pieces of a broken comet strike the planet's atmosphere. Earth-based telescopes and spacecraft nearby Jupiter took pictures of huge, bright fireballs as the comet pieces entered the planet's atmosphere. Dark, circular blobs formed where the fragments hit—some of which lasted for more than a year.

HIT FROM ABOVE ◄

You may now be asking, "What happens if a small asteroid strays from the asteroid belt?" It's true. An asteroid could eventually cross the path of a planet or moon in the solar system. If this occurs at the right moment, there would be a collision. Such strikes have happened to all the planets and moons in the solar system at some time in the past. How do we know it happened on Mercury, Venus, Mars, and even on the Martian moons, Phobos and Deimos? Because there are huge craters on these solar system bodies. Most of these craters were caused by asteroid strikes over the past 4.6 billion years, or since the solar system was born.

By this time, you may be wondering about the Earth. Could an asteroid strike our home planet? Scientists realize asteroids can come very close—and even strike the Earth. Over billions of years, asteroids have crashed into our planet. The evidence is clear. So far, more than 150 impact craters, or huge holes in the ground caused by falling space objects, have been discovered on the Earth. You may have visited one of the youngest craters that formed only about 49,000 years ago, called Meteor Crater, near Winslow Arizona. This roughly three-quarters-of-a-mile hole (1.2 kilometers) formed when an asteroid about 75 feet (23 meters) wide slammed into the surface. Luckily, no such craters have formed in recent years—and so far, no asteroids look as if they will strike the Earth anytime soon.

ASTEROID SHOWERS ◄

There's something a bit scary about visiting the asteroids— especially since you found out that they can wander away from the asteroid belt. In fact, if we think back to Earth, we

free asteroid shower

know that large and small dinosaurs lived on our planet for millions of years—and then disappeared. Some scientists believe that around 65 million years ago, a shower of asteroids and/or comets struck the Earth. As the huge chunks of rock and ice fell on our planet, dust and debris flew into the air. The dust was soon carried around the Earth, blocking out much of the Sun's bright light and heat. The temperatures changed all over the Earth, along with the vegetation. Because the dinosaurs could not adapt to the changes, they eventually became extinct.

Could this theory be true? Some astronomers say yes; others say that events such as huge volcanic eruptions helped wipe out the dinosaurs before the asteroids hit—or both occurred together, causing the extinctions. Scientists believe something catastrophic occurred—and it probably had to do with space objects striking the Earth. After all, we have been struck in the past by asteroids and comets. Just look at Meteor Crater in Arizona, or the Sudbury Basin in Canada—only two of the more than 150 such impact craters on Earth.

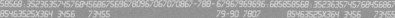

FIFTH STOP: JUPITER

FIFTH STOP: JUPITER

et's head for Jupiter, the fifth planet in the solar system. You'll be amazed at the planet's size. It is the largest planet in the solar system and is eleven times the Earth's diameter. You could fit more than 1,300 Earths inside this planet. In fact, Jupiter is so large that every planet in the solar system could fit inside and there would still be room for more. If you traveled around the circumference of Jupiter at 6 miles (10 kilometers) per hour, it would take you 1,935 days to finish your trip. On Earth, such a trip would only take 173 days.

THE WEATHER OUT HERE

On this planet, you'll quickly realize that you're not near Earth anymore. Jupiter takes about 12 Earth years to spin around the Sun. In fact, if you were 10 Earth years old, you would not have even celebrated your first Jupiter birthday. But the days would go fast—a Jupiter day only lasts on average 10 Earth hours, so you'd better plan the day's activities carefully.

The Great Red Spot

What will you see when you look at Jupiter's atmosphere? As you get closer to the planet, you can see the rapid movement of colorful gases within the clouds. The planet is like a huge cloud machine. The air is mostly hydrogen and helium, with other gases giving the clouds their characteristic pastel and deep, rich colors. The planet produces more heat than it receives from the Sun, causing the clouds to violently churn and move quickly across the planet.

One fun activity on Jupiter is watching the lightning. Swift-moving clouds often carry crackling arcs of lightning. On Earth, lightning is created by colliding water and ice droplets in thunderstorm clouds—and it may form the same way in Jupiter's clouds that contain water ice. If you could stand in a lightning-filled area on the gas giant, you would be astounded at how much brighter the lightning flashes are than they are on Earth.

And don't pass up the main attraction on this gas giant—the Great Red Spot, a giant "storm" that has been taking place on Jupiter for more than 300 years. If you look closely, you'll notice that this bright red spot is just under two times the diameter of the Earth; it measured around three Earth diameters about a century ago, which means it's shrinking. The spot is surrounded by wispy swirls of clouds in almost every possible shade of orange, blue, green, and yellow. And scientists are discovering that more great storms may be forming all the time.

NO PLACE TO WALK

What will you experience when you travel through Jupiter's atmosphere? As on all the planets so far, don't forget your pressurized, heated spacesuit. The upper cloud layers are the coldest, measuring around –238 degrees Fahrenheit (–150 degrees Celsius). Deeper in the atmosphere, it warms to around 68 degrees Fahrenheit (20 degrees Celsius), close to the average temperature on our own planet. As you make your way toward the middle of the planet, it becomes darker and even warmer—with the pressure increasing to unbearable levels.

In fact, Jupiter has a big surprise. Unlike the Earth and the other inner planets of the solar system, Jupiter has no solid surface crust. The gases just get thicker until, deep into the atmosphere, a liquid hydrogen layer is reached. Moving even closer to the center, the enormous pressures create a

While Jupiter is certainly worth stopping off at, the real highlights here are its four main moons—Ganymede, Callisto, Io, and Europa.

rocky core of iron and other lighter materials. You may have to go all the way to the center of this giant planet before your feet can reach even the most insignificant piece of solid footing.

If you could somehow stand on this core, your arms would feel heavier than lead. The extreme gravity would make your legs buckle. It would feel like walking around with a hump-back whale on your back. And if you could walk on Jupiter, you would weigh a great deal more than on Earth. In fact, a 100 pound (45.36 kilogram) person on Earth would weigh 253.3 pounds (114.89 kilograms) on Jupiter.

As you back away from the gas giant, you can see several small, faint rings circling the planet—made up of dust particles. How did the rings form? Could they be the remains of a moon ripped apart by the gravity of Jupiter and its larger moons? No one truly knows.

WHAT A HOT SPOT

Jupiter may not be much to visit, but its moons are a definite must-see. You'd better watch your approach to the first moon you'll visit—it's the most geologically active in the solar system. It is called Io, and it is known for throwing volcanic material into space. Although it is one of the larger moons around the planet Jupiter, Io is only a little bigger

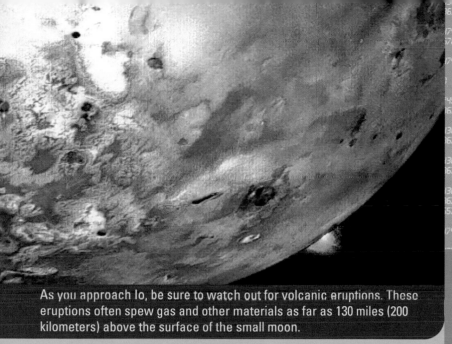

As you approach Io, be sure to watch out for volcanic eruptions. These eruptions often spew gas and other materials as far as 130 miles (200 kilometers) above the surface of the small moon.

than our own Moon. It moves quickly, taking just over a day and a half to travel around the giant planet.

People who take this tour often call Io a "giant pizza." That's because the moon's face is covered with light and dark spots—a mix of yellow, orange, red, and dark brown, mostly caused by sulfur. The sulfur should be white, but the heat from the volcanic activity turns it different colors.

You'll soon notice this "pizza" is not quiet—it's like a restless sleeper, always in motion. Why? Because sometimes the moon is being pulled in the direction

The surface of Io is an excellent place to see volcanic eruptions up close, as with this eruption in an area called Tvashtar Catena.

of its nearest neighbor, the moon Europa, while at other times it's being yanked toward its mother planet, Jupiter. In other words, Io is slowly being torn apart.

Make sure your spacesuit is in working order here. Because of the volcanic activity, some of the hottest temperatures in the solar system (outside of the Sun) are found here—and yet most of the surface is bitterly cold. In areas lacking volcanoes, the surface temperatures are about –243 degrees Fahrenheit (–153 degrees Celsius). Even though it is cold, your spacesuit will also have to be heat-resistant to walk on Io's surface. Why? Because the many volcanoes heat up the surrounding area. In fact, if you weren't wearing a space suit and you stood at certain spots on Io, one side of your body would burn while the other side froze—both at the same time.

Don't forget your camera when you come to this moon. Volcanic eruptions of hot lava (or liquid rock) are

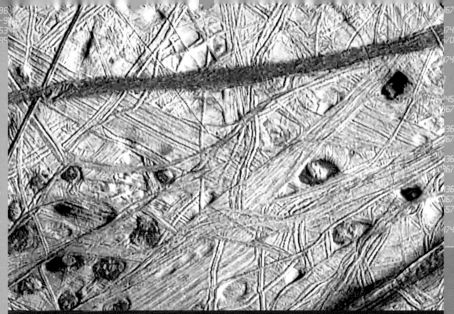

Before leaving the Galilean satellites, be sure to check out the "freckles" and shallow pits on Europa's northern hemisphere. Scientists believe that these may have been caused by water welling up below the ice-covered surface.

everywhere—and nothing like those on Earth. As you look around, you'll no doubt see giant plumes of rock, dust, and sulfur dioxide gas from multiple volcanoes across the landscape. Since Io is small and does not have much gravity, these mushroom-shaped plumes rise to great heights— up to 130 miles (210 kilometers) into the sky. If a geyser the size of Yellowstone National Park's "Old Faithful" erupted on Io, it would create a plume 22 miles (35 kilometers) high. Because of this volcanic activity, Io generates electric power—about as much energy as 100 electric power stations on Earth.

QUIET AND ICY

Io may be an eye-catching sight, but don't forget to visit some of Jupiter's other moons—all with unique attractions. Besides Io, there are three other large moons. These giant, icy moons all share one fascinating thing in common. They may all have water oceans beneath their icy crusts.

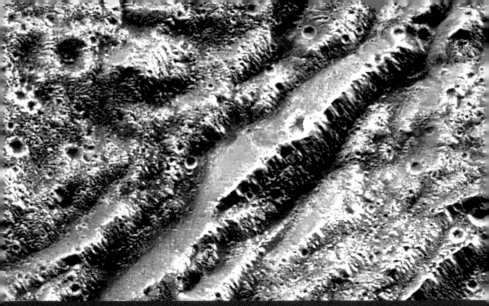

The surface of Ganymede is covered with long ridges, like these, which form a series of "stair steps," like a tilted stack of books.

Just take a step on Ganymede, the largest satellite in the solar system (about as large as Mercury)—and of course, Jupiter's largest moon. The icy surface has dark patches covered with craters, and large, light-colored cracks—many hundreds of miles long. They probably formed when an asteroid or comet crashed into the moon, similar to the way thin ice covering a puddle on Earth cracks when you walk on it.

Next check out Jupiter's second largest moon, Callisto—the most cratered moon in the solar system. By far one of the most interesting places to visit on the large moon is Valhalla Basin, a circular area about 373 miles (600 kilometers across). From above, it is surrounded by 15 rings that look like ripples that form when you drop a stone into a pond.

Without a doubt, your next stop should be the satellite Europa. Here, your space boots will crack and crunch on the thick ice. Europa is just a little smaller than our own Moon and, unlike most members of the solar system, it has very few craters. Instead, it is covered with ice and crisscrossed by dark cracks. How did the cracks form? One idea is that

Europa's underground oceans swell from Jupiter's very powerful gravitational pull. This puts stress on the ocean waters, causing the ice covering the moon to move and eventually crack. These cracks are soon filled with upwelling water and slush—like toothpaste being squeezed from a tube—which in turn freeze almost instantly.

The oceans on Europa are of special interest to scientists as compared to its sister moons, Ganymede and Callisto. The main reason is that based on recent measurements, Europa may have oceans as deep as 100 miles (160 kilometers). In fact, Europa probably has more water than the Earth, even though it is about one-fourth as wide as our planet. Furthermore, there appears to be a brown layer of film on the underside of the icy crust. Some scientists believe it could be evidence of organic compounds in the oceans—but no one knows for sure. So like our oceans on Earth, Europa may have some form of life swimming in its depths. The life forms probably wouldn't be like the fish we eat on Earth, but might be similar to the creatures that exist without light from the Sun, which we've recently found deep in our oceans. On Europa, life forms would also be without sunlight—using the heat from within the moon to live.

Thanks to the Galileo spacecraft that flew around Jupiter, we now know that there are at least 63 smaller moons orbiting the planet. As you visit the other moons you'll notice that some spin close to Jupiter, while others are in distant orbits—all dancing around the gas giant like a miniature solar system. Many of the moons are strangely shaped, much like the irregular asteroids in the asteroid belt. But no one really knows where the moons originated. Guesses range from captured asteroids from the asteroid belt to a possible huge moon that broke apart by Jupiter's gravity.

You may wonder if there is life on Jupiter or some of its moons. Who knows? Would a creature on Jupiter be as flat

FIFTH STOP: JUPITER

as a pancake because of the planet's great gravity? Or would it be a wispy creature, blown from place to place by wind currents—the way jellyfish are pushed by Earth's ocean currents? Could something live under the icy crust of Europa or along the heated volcanoes of Io? Your guess is as good as anyone else's!

THE GALILEAN SATELLITES

It's nice to visit Jupiter's four largest moons close up—but you may wonder, "Can they can be seen from Earth?" Yes, they can—and they were discovered by the Italian astronomer Galileo Galilei. In 1610, Galileo noted the moons Io, Ganymede, Callisto, and Europa through his crude telescope. Because of this, astronomers refer to these moons as the Galilean satellites. Back on Earth, if you observe Jupiter with binoculars or a small telescope, you'll see these moons to the right and left of the planet, their order depending on the night. And if you watch them night after night, you'll see how they change positions as they spin around Jupiter.

SHINING JUPITER?

Here's a tour puzzle. Can you imagine what it would be like to have two stars in our sky? At one time, some scientists believed it could have happened—and that Jupiter could have been another "sun" in our solar system. But in order for Jupiter to have been a star, it would have had to be much more massive than it is—more than sixty times as large as it is today. Then huge pressure (due to gravity) would have started thermonuclear fusion reactions in its core—the activity that allows our Sun to shine. The solar system would then have had two stars, which is a commonly observed occurrence in other parts of our galaxy. But then again, with two such stars, who knows how life on Earth would have evolved, or if it would have existed at all.

SIXTH STOP: SATURN

SIXTH STOP: SATURN

Our next stop is Saturn, the second largest planet in the solar system and the sixth one from the Sun. You can immediately see why most people call it the major attraction of the solar system tour. It has the largest, most beautiful set of rings of all the planets.

Don't forget your camera here, either. Not only are the rings worth a picture, so are the pastel-colored clouds that cover the planet. Saturn's interior is much like Jupiter's—all gases and no real surface. Because Saturn is mostly gas, it is not very dense—in fact, it is less dense than water. If you could find a water-filled bathtub that was big enough, the whole planet would easily float.

WHAT'S IN THE AIR?

Take a look around you. Hopefully, you packed something sturdy to hold on to because Saturn's winds move rapidly around the planet—in some places, up to 1,000 miles (1,600 kilometers) per hour. If you faced the same wind speeds on Earth, very little would be left standing.

The planet's weather is changeable, too. The atmosphere has a few storms that seem to stay in one place, although they are not as large or constant as Jupiter's Great Red Spot. But giant storms can also pop up suddenly on the planet. One place you'll want to be sure to check out is a large, white storm that appeared about 60 years ago, disappeared a few years later, then recently came back again.

Don't bother taking off your spacesuit helmet while you're here—the air isn't breathable. Saturn's air is mostly hydrogen and helium, although there are other gases that give the clouds their characteristic light, pastel colors.

Storm on Saturn

If you stay long enough on the planet, you'll soon see that Saturn is like Jupiter in many ways. Like Jupiter, Saturn's atmosphere has enormous winds. Saturn's lower layers are also under great pressure—close to ten million times the pressure on Earth. Saturn also spins rapidly, with the day lasting just over 10 Earth hours.

But there are also major differences between the two giant gas planets. Saturn is much farther from the Sun than Jupiter, taking 29½ years to orbit our star compared to Jupiter's 12 years. And contrary to what you'd think, if you could somehow stand on Saturn, you would weigh close to what you weigh on Earth. A person who is 100 pounds (45.36 kilograms) on Earth would weigh 106 pounds (48.08 kilograms) on Saturn. This is because, although the planet is huge, it has less gravitational pull than Jupiter.

Of course, the biggest difference between Jupiter and Saturn—and the planet's real attraction—are the beautiful rings around Saturn. As you approach, you can see they are actually made up of thousands of rings. Some of the rings are braided, with small satellites trapped inside. The entire ring system is wide—about two-thirds the distance between the Earth and the Moon—but they average less than 10 miles (16 kilometers) thick. You may want your sunglasses as you look at the rings. They are very bright because the icy particles reflect the Sun's light—the way snow and ice reflect the sunlight on Earth.

Saturn's rings

From a distance, you'll think the rings look solid. But get a bit closer and you'll see that they're made up of chunks of ice, rock, and dust. If you go through the rings, you'll want to watch out—some icy rocks are the size of a house; others are no larger than your thumbnail. These chunks all travel

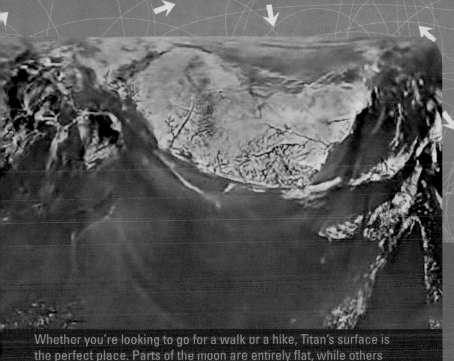

Whether you're looking to go for a walk or a hike, Titan's surface is the perfect place. Parts of the moon are entirely flat, while others are incredibly hilly and mountainous.

slowly around the planet, with only Saturn's gravity keeping them from drifting off into space.

About now, you may wonder how Saturn's rings formed. No one knows for sure. Some astronomers believe the rings are debris left over from a broken moon—torn apart by the gravitational pull of Saturn. As the moon orbited the planet, it was pushed and pulled until, after thousands of years, it shattered into pieces. Other astronomers believe the rings formed as the solar system was born around 4.6 billion years ago. As loose material spun around Saturn, some of the larger moons like Iapetus and Titan formed. But one moon did not form. Instead, the material spread out around the planet, forming the beautiful rings we see today.

SATURN'S BIGGEST MOON

If you have an extra day, a side trip to Saturn's moon Titan would be well worth your time. This giant moon is larger

Initially thought to be rocks or ice blocks, the objects shown here are actually small pebbles. It was likely one of these pebbles that Huygens first probed when it landed on the surface of Saturn's moon Titan.

than our own Moon—and even the planets Mercury and Pluto, which means there are plenty of features to explore. Titan's atmosphere is made up mostly of nitrogen, just as on Earth, but you still won't be able to breathe freely on Titan. The atmosphere is mostly void of oxygen and contains gases that are poisonous to human life.

What else do we know about Titan? In 2005, a small probe dropped through the atmosphere of the moon. The probe, called the Huygens, came from the Cassini spacecraft and took measurements and images of the moon as it fell through the atmosphere. The craft found that the temperature on Titan was a brisk –290 degrees Fahrenheit (–179 degrees Celsius)—so make sure you bring along an extra sweater or two.

The pictures sent back by the craft were amazing. Thanks to Huygens, you can now add the exploration of Titan's many riverbeds and shorelines to your itinerary. One interesting thing to note as you explore the surface of this moon is that the riverbeds and shorelines were not carved by water, but by methane rains. There are even dark, splotchy methane lakes around the pole regions—including one as large as Earth's Lake Ontario in central North America.

The ground here is also interesting to examine. Based on the Huygens initial findings, it seemed to be a thin, frozen crust over a smoother, softer layer. But after considerable research, scientists found that a sensor on the probe hit a pebble and then pushed it aside before landing on the slushy surface. Scientists now believe that Titan probably has a water ocean that is kept liquid by ammonia, much the way antifreeze works in our cars. And this ocean lies underneath a crust covered by hydrocarbon sludge.

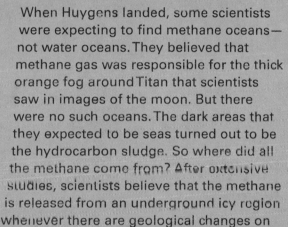

When Huygens landed, some scientists were expecting to find methane oceans— not water oceans. They believed that methane gas was responsible for the thick orange fog around Titan that scientists saw in images of the moon. But there were no such oceans. The dark areas that they expected to be seas turned out to be the hydrocarbon sludge. So where did all the methane come from? After extensive studies, scientists believe that the methane is released from an underground icy region whenever there are geological changes on the moon. These changes may have happened three times in the moon's history. The third change, which began 500 million years ago, may still be going on today.

But don't think methane isn't important on this moon. Through further research of Titan's climate, scientists have determined that it does in fact rain methane on Titan. Although it does not happen often, the occasional rains apparently leave temporary rivers and pools of methane. But these seemingly disappear quickly—and no one really knows how or why this happens.

Don't leave Mimas without taking a look at its one large crater, Herschel. At 80 miles (130 kilometers) wide, Herschel is almost one-third the size of the small moon.

Look around. Did you notice the other 56 or so moons orbiting Saturn? They are the ones we can see, but there are probably more hidden in Saturn's ring system. These moons are much smaller than Titan and do not have atmospheres. Some are dark, some are light, and some are trapped in Saturn's rings. Many of the moons are lined with grooves or marked by craters. They may be all that's left of a larger moon that split apart in a huge collision. Or they may have formed when the solar system began. One thing's for sure. A day on any of Saturn's moons would be time well spent.

Many of the moons are particularly striking, especially if you like to hike and climb. Rhea, the second largest moon of Saturn, measures 950 miles (1,530 kilometers) in diameter and is covered with craters. Tethys is 670 miles (1,080 kilometers) in diameter. It also has one huge ice trench that is well worth visiting—the Ithaca Chasma, which measures

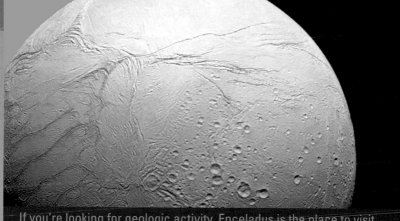

If you're looking for geologic activity, Enceladus is the place to visit. The moon's surface is covered with fractures, folds, ridges, and craters. "Cold geysers" often shoot water vapor as far as 250 miles (400 kilometers) above the surface of the moon.

40 miles (65 kilometers) wide and extends over three-quarters of the way around the moon.

There's also a small chunk of rock called Mimas that measures about 260 miles (420 kilometers) in diameter. It has a large crater called Herschel on its surface that measures 80 miles (130 kilometers) wide. In fact, climbers would like the crater's central mountain, as it rises higher than the Earth's tallest mountain—Mt. Everest.

There are other small moons to investigate as well. Iapetus is one of Saturn's smaller satellites. It is dark and rocky on one side, and white and icy on the other. Hyperion is a battered piece of rock that may be left over from a larger moon that once circled Saturn.

Now take a look at that relatively smaller moon orbiting rather close to Saturn. It is called Enceladus, and at first glance, it doesn't seem that special. It has some areas covered with small craters—and other areas with no craters at all. But if you take a closer look, you'll see that Enceladus is white, reflecting almost 100 percent of the sunlight that strikes it. Because of this and Enceladus' distance from the Sun, temperatures only reach around –330 degrees Fahrenheit

(–201 degrees Celsius), so turn up your spacesuit heater. If you look up, you may also notice a faint dust cloud above the planet. Scientists believe these dust particles may somehow be associated with one of Saturn's rings.

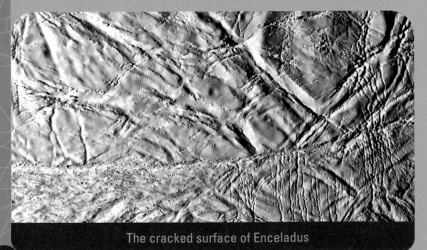

The cracked surface of Enceladus

If you walk around the surface of Enceladus, you'll see cracked and deformed terrain, but there are also flat plains that hint to scientists that there may be water underneath the icy crust. But if it is so cold on the moon, how can there be liquid water? The answer may be the volcano-like plumes of water vapor and ice that often jet from the moon's surface, reaching almost 250 miles (400 kilometers) into space. Scientists still don't know how the moon generates enough heat to form these "cold" geysers—and keep the water liquid. Much like Io, one of Jupiter's moons, Enceladus may be heated on the inside from the immense pull of its giant parent planet, Saturn. Little did you know when you started this tour that geologic activity played such a major role in our solar system!

On your tour of the moons, don't leave out Phoebe—a moon that is only 120 miles (200 kilometers) in diameter and is farthest from Saturn. Because it is so far from the planet, it takes Phoebe about a year and a half to orbit Saturn. But there is something else weird about this small moon. For some unknown reason, it orbits Saturn in a direction opposite to that of the other moons.

LIFE ON THE RINGED PLANET

Will you observe life on Saturn or one of its moons? Probably not. But there is a wild chance that Titan may be one of the few places in the solar system that has life. Why? Because Titan's atmosphere has hydrocarbon compounds that may include the building blocks of life. It also has a mixture of gases—including nitrogen, ammonia, water, methane, and ethane—that could sustain life. Who knows? Could these gases combine to produce a livable atmosphere, much like on early Earth? The life might not look like giraffes, bears, beavers, cats, dogs, or even penguins—it's just too cold on Titan for such creatures to develop. But it may hold smaller life forms, like bacteria—or a life form we have never seen before.

SEVENTH STOP: URANUS

SEVENTH STOP: URANUS

Speeding your way through the outer solar system, you may notice a pale greenish object in the darkness. It is the seventh planet from the Sun and well worth the visit. Uranus, with its at least 27 moons is a planet that also has many strange cloud features in its atmosphere.

STRANGELY SPINNING PLANET

If you look very closely, you can see banded patterns of clouds on Uranus, much like a faint version of Saturn's atmosphere. Uranus's atmosphere is made up of hydrogen, helium, and methane gases. So why is most of the planet a greenish-blue color? When the Sun's light strikes the methane gases in the planet's atmosphere, it absorbs red light and we see the green. But if you visit the south pole of Uranus, you better bring a flash for your camera. This part of the planet is dark and surrounded by a broad band of reddish-brown clouds.

If you waited for Uranus to travel once around the Sun, you would be there a long time—close to 84 Earth years. This means that it would take 84 Earth years to become one Uranus year old. But your days on the planet would go fast—close to 18 Earth hours. And after spending just one day on Uranus, you'd definitely notice something strange. The Sun rises in the west and sets in the east. In other words, the planet rotates " backward" (or retrograde) from what you are used to seeing on Earth. If you could step back and see the whole planet,

Unlike other planets, Uranus rolls along on its side.

you would notice that it tips in a strange way. Instead of spinning like the Earth, Uranus spins at right angles to the Sun, like a ball rolling across a smooth surface. This means that each pole of Uranus experiences 21 years of daylight and 21 years of darkness. Whatever you do, don't forget to turn up the heater in your spacesuit. That's because Uranus is not only one of the coldest planets in the solar system (the temperature can dip to −362 degrees Fahrenheit [−219 degrees Celsius]), but the one with the longest winters and summers. You'll definitely need more than thermal underwear there.

Go ahead; don't be shy. Weigh yourself on Uranus. Did you notice that your weight is not much different from your weight on Earth? In fact, if you weigh 100 pounds (45.36 kilograms) on Earth, you'll weigh 88.9 pounds (40.32 kilograms) on Uranus. This is because like Saturn, the planet is big but its gravitation pull is not great.

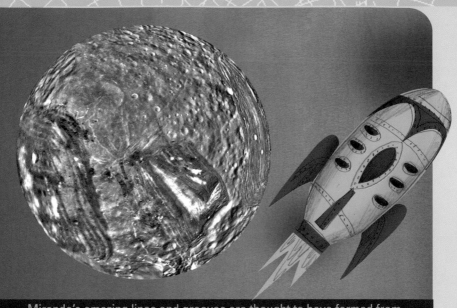

Miranda's amazing lines and grooves are thought to have formed from the splitting and reforming of its surface after being hit by objects from space.

WHO THREW THIS MOON AROUND?

Don't forget to take a side trip to Uranus's moon Miranda, the closest satellite orbiting the planet. This small moon—about half the size of Uranus's other satellites—is one of the roughest and most irregular members of the solar system. It's definitely an ideal place to explore—it looks as if it was twisted and turned by some unknown hand trying to work with clay. You may want to take a few day trips to Miranda's craters, many that look like those on our Moon, or maybe to the deep canyons, many ten times deeper than the Earth's Grand Canyon in Arizona. The moon also has strangely shaped grooves that look like a series of roads, and even one feature shaped like a boomerang. Don't forget your camera. You're not likely to have this opportunity again.

You're no doubt curious as to how these strange shapes developed. Scientists believe Miranda was struck by huge space objects many times in its history. It broke apart, but

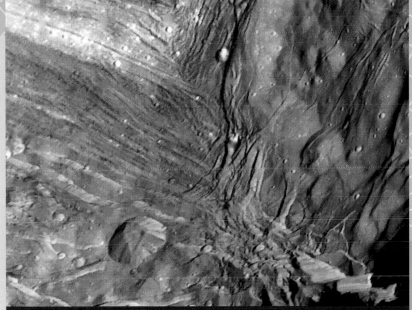

You may need a few days to see all the sights on Miranda, such as the moon's many grooves and craters. It is believed that this strangely shaped moon was torn apart and then pulled back together by gravity.

then gravity pulled it back together. Looking at its amazing lines and grooves, scientists think it may have split and reformed as many as five times.

You'll probably want to check out the other moons around Uranus, too. From Earth, you would barely see the five brightest moons through a telescope. But close up on this tour, you can see all of them. Ariel and Miranda are younger moons that orbit close to Uranus; Oberon, Unbriel, and Titania are older moons orbiting farther out. Titania is also Uranus's largest moon, with long valleys and many small craters. Oberon has many small craters surrounded by bright rays. As the craters formed, tons of rock and debris flew into the sky and then gradually fell to the ground, creating the rays. As you can see, dark material has also oozed from the bottom of these craters.

Look around a bit more. You can probably see that many smaller moons spin around the pale, greenish-blue planet,

2 p.m.

Oberon is just one of the outer moons orbiting Uranus

all with dark surfaces. Most of the tiny moons are less than 100 miles (161 kilometers) across, and may be captured asteroids or fragments of a once-whole moon.

WHAT ELSE IS OUT THERE?

Like all the other outer planets (except Pluto), if you look at Uranus with the Sun in the background, you will see rings. Before the Voyager 2 spacecraft flew by the planet in the mid-1980s, scientists believed there were nine rings. Taking a closer look, you can see that there are actually 11 main rings—the majority of them measuring only about 6 miles (10 kilometers) wide. The ring region is filled with ice, rocks, and dust, with some particles only a few tenths of an

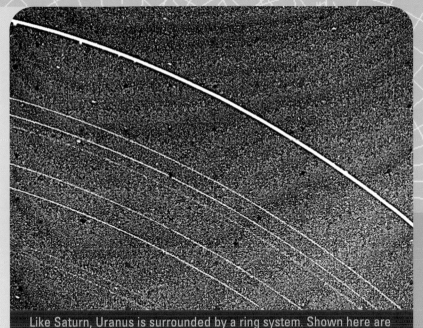

Like Saturn, Uranus is surrounded by a ring system. Shown here are the planet's nine faint, narrow rings.

inch in diameter. They also are very dark—which is why they are difficult to see from Earth—so take a picture to prove to your friends that the rings do exist.

Will you find life on Uranus or its moons? There is probably no life on the small moons because they don't seem to have atmospheres. But is there life on the planet? Probably not. If life were to exist on Uranus, it would have to endure bitter cold and be able to breathe hydrogen, helium, and many poisonous gases.

HOW ARE THEY NAMED?

By now, after all the places you've encountered on the tour, you're probably wondering how all the moons, craters, and features of the solar system are named. Most of the time, they are named after famous people and characters from well-known books or ancient legends. For example, the craters and features on Venus are named after women, such

Belinda

Rosalind

Caliban

Ariel

Sycorax

Puck

as Aphrodite, a mythological goddess. Uranus's satellites are named after characters from William Shakespeare's and Alexander Pope's works, such as Miranda from Shakespeare's *The Tempest*.

Asteroids and comets are named a bit differently. In most cases, the asteroid is named at the request of the discoverer. One scientist even named an asteroid Spock, after his cat. Comets are named after their discoverer. Often times, a comet has two names because it was discovered by two people. For example, Comet Hale-Bopp was named after astronomer Alan Hale and amateur astronomer Thomas Bopp, who both independently found the comet at the same time.

EIGHTH STOP: NEPTUNE

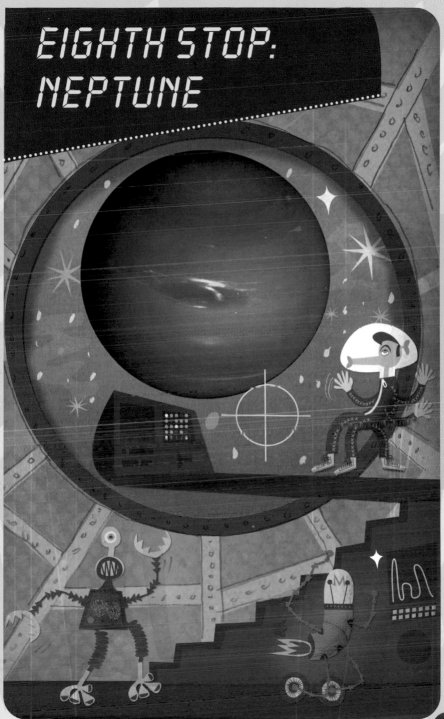

EIGHTH STOP: NEPTUNE

rab your camera again. You're about to visit one of the more colorful planets in the outer solar system—the pale, bluish-green planet Neptune. As you can see, it has broad bands in different shades of blue and bright polar regions. Let's hope your camera comes with a flash, because the sunlight here is about nine hundred times dimmer than on Earth. In fact, if you look back at the Sun from Neptune, Earth looks like a flashlight beam seen from 900 feet (274 meters) away.

THE BLUISH PLANET

If you stay long on the planet, you'll notice that the days go fast. In fact, it takes only 19 Earth hours to complete a Neptune day. But your years would drag. If you sat and waited for a year to go by on Neptune, you would be sitting for 168 Earth years. While you're waiting, don't forget to keep your spacesuit on because the atmosphere is filled with hydrogen, helium, methane, and ammonia—gases you can't breathe. Keep the suit's heater on, too—the temperature averages about –353 degrees Fahrenheit (–178 degrees Celsius). And you won't need a rope here like on an asteroid. If you weigh 100 pounds (45.36 kilograms) on Earth, you'll weigh 112.5 pounds (51.03 kilograms) on Neptune.

While you're here you'll definitely want to see one of Neptune's main attractions—the spots in the planet's clouds. These are great storms that seem to change over time. When Voyager 2 visited the planet in the late 1980s, it took pictures of several storms—the Great Dark Spot, the Small Dark Spot, and a bright "Scooter," all moving across the surface at different speeds. In fact, Neptune's winds blew the Great Dark Spot westward at 700 miles per hour (300 meters per second). In 1994, observations by the Hubble Space Telescope showed that the Great Dark Spot had disappeared, with new light and dark spots forming elsewhere.

WINDY DAYS

Hold on to your hat—and your spacesuit's helmet! Neptune's winds are the fastest in the solar system, often reaching 1,243 miles (2,000 kilometers) per hour. The most rapid winds are found only in certain parts of the planet's atmosphere. But there seem to be changes in store for the planet's clouds. In recent years, pictures from the Hubble Space Telescope have shown that Neptune is getting cloudier.

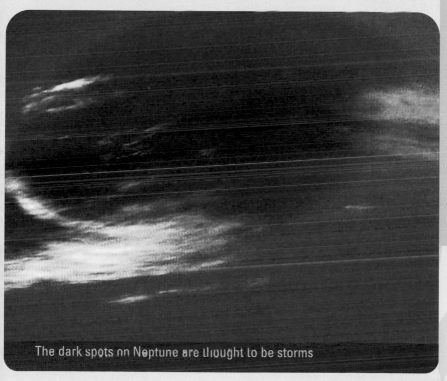

The dark spots on Neptune are thought to be storms

Scientists believe this is because the planet's orbit is quite elliptical (or oval)—and it is getting closer to the Sun. The clouds are probably increasing because the atmosphere's temperature is rising.

From the right angle, you'll be able to see Neptune's ring system. Here it is backlit by the Sun.

RINGS, OF COURSE

Before you leave Neptune, take time and look over your shoulder. Like the other outer planets of the solar system, Neptune has rings—two main rings, a fuzzy ring closer to the planet, and two that are difficult to see even close up. You may want to take a picture, as Neptune's rings are so dark and thin that you can't see them without the Sun in the background. They are so thin, in fact, that astronomers first believed the rings were incomplete, forming arcs instead of whole rings. Thanks to spacecraft images, they now know that the rings extend all the way around the planet—and that the brighter areas of the rings are just clumps of particles.

Are you going to find life on Neptune? It's possible, but the chances are slim. There is so little heat and sunlight on the planet. And the gases in the atmosphere are poisonous to life as we know it.

ARE THEY REALLY TWINS?

Did you ever hear that Neptune is considered Uranus's twin? Both planets are about the same size and similar in color. Both have an atmosphere filled with hydrogen, helium, and methane. Neptune has rings, and so does Uranus. Both have a combination of larger and smaller moons. And maybe the two gas planets formed in the same way.

But as you probably noticed in your travels, there are plenty of differences between the two planets. For instance, Neptune has more cloud features in its atmosphere than Uranus. Neptune emits more heat than Uranus. It takes Neptune over 168 years to spin around the Sun compared to Uranus's 84 years. Neptune's gravity is also greater than that of Uranus. Add Neptune's greater distance from the Sun's warmth—and maybe these two planets are not really twins after all.

MIXED UP MOON

You can't really leave Neptune without a visit to its remarkable moon Triton. At about 1,690 miles (2,720 kilometers) in diameter, Triton is approximately the same size as nearby Pluto. It travels around Neptune in close to six days—but it spins in the opposite direction from the other moons around the planet. It's a great moon to explore and you'll want to stop at some of the frozen lakes, craters of varying sizes, and vast cracks in its surface. More importantly, you'll want to spend some time watching the tall geysers that spew out nitrogen frost and other material. Triton is the coldest body in the solar system that has geologic activity. Just imagine, a place so cold that liquid nitrogen is actually considered a "boiling" substance, like lava on Earth!

Here, too, you definitely want to keep the heater on "high" in your spacesuit because Triton's average temperature is almost –400 degrees Fahrenheit (–240 degrees Celsius).

Looking around, you may notice that the cracks in the
moon's surface look as if they've been filled with ice. Triton
also looks as if it is split in two. One part is pinkish and
bright where the polar cap coats almost half the surface
with methane-ice; the other part is darker where its nitrogen,
carbon dioxide, and water-ice crust is exposed. In fact, part
of the moon's rough covering has often been compared to
the skin of a cantaloupe.

But you'll notice that this moon is also different. Triton is the
only Neptune moon with an atmosphere. Its thin air is made
up of nitrogen and a trace of methane. In fact, it is one of
only three bodies in the solar system to have a mostly nitrogen
atmosphere. If you look closely, you can see a layer of haze
above the atmosphere, composed of ice or other particles
such as methane. The moon also has very low pressure at

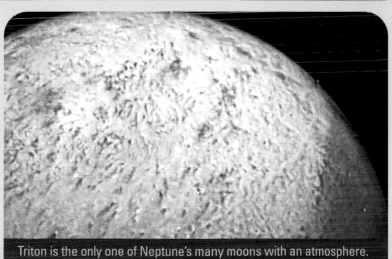

Triton is the only one of Neptune's many moons with an atmosphere. The atmosphere is made up of nitrogen and methane, though, so you'll want to make sure to wear your spacesuit when you visit.

its surface—seventy thousand times lower than on Earth. Scientists believe that Triton was not originally one of Neptune's moons, but rather a body known as a Kuiper Belt object. It is believed that Neptune captured the body, pulling it into the planet's orbit and making it one of its moons.

After spending the day exploring the wonders of Triton, you'll find very little of interest to visit on Neptune's other moons. That's because the other twelve moons nearby are small, irregular in shape, and probably look a great deal like asteroids.

NINTH STOP: PLUTO

It is difficult to know much about the surface of Pluto. Viewing the surface detail has been compared to trying to read the printing on a gold ball located 33 miles (55 kilometers) away! (So be sure to bring your binoculars.)

NINTH STOP: PLUTO

I t's time for you to travel to the last (and smallest) planet in the solar system. You're now at Pluto, a planet that lies about 3,666 million miles (5,900 million kilometers) from the Sun. In fact, it is so distant that it would take you 10 years to travel to Pluto from Earth by today's spacecraft.

FAR FROM HOME

The first thing you'll notice when you arrive on Pluto is that you need a lantern. The light is very dim—almost like a moonlit night back on Earth. In fact, the Sun's light is around a thousand times dimmer on the small planet than on Earth. The second thing you'll notice is the spinning of the planet—it turns in the opposite direction of the Earth (or retrograde), with the pinpoint of the Sun setting in the east and rising in the west.

On the tour, you'll also notice that Pluto is only about two-thirds the size of the Earth's Moon and is truly a dark, icy planet. In fact, if you weighed 100 pounds (45.36 kilograms) on Earth, you would only weigh 6.7 pounds (3.04 kilograms) on Pluto. Most people would be amazed at how high they could jump on Pluto because there is little gravity holding them to the planet. You may want to grab your camera and ask someone to take a picture of your high jump!

WILD PLANET

If you stayed a while on Pluto, you'd notice that it has one of the strangest orbits on our tour. In 1979, the small planet moved inside the orbit of its nearest neighbor, Neptune. That meant that Neptune was the farthest planet from the Sun—at least until 1999 when Pluto moved outside the orbit of Neptune and reclaimed its status as the farthest planet.

Pluto and its moon Charon have often been considered a double planet system, although both objects are currently being considered dwarf planets.

Pluto travels in a crazy orbit around the Sun, taking 248 years to complete an orbit. In other words, if you were 10 Earth years old, you would only be 0.04 Pluto years old. You would have to wait 248 years to be 1 Pluto year old—giving you plenty of time to plan your first birthday party.

Again, your spacesuit becomes useful on this planet. The warmest temperature on Pluto is about –350 degrees Fahrenheit (–212 degrees Celsius). A thin, hazy atmosphere of nitrogen blankets the planet. As you can see, most of the surface is covered by nitrogen and methane ice that shows up as bright spots on the planet's surface (ice is a great reflector of light). There are also water and ammonia ices present, and there may be rock under the surface. In other words, it appears that Pluto is a small, orbiting chunk of rock and ice.

TINY MOON AROUND A TINY PLANET

Pluto is the smallest planet to have a moon. It's an amazing sight to see on our tour—like looking at a ping-pong ball going around a basketball. Pluto's companion moon,

Charon, was discovered in 1978, at the Lowell Observatory in Arizona—the same place in which Pluto was discovered in 1930. Charon is half the size of Pluto, and many astronomers call Pluto-Charon a double-planet system. In fact, since the turn of the century, two more very tiny moons have been discovered as well—called Nix and Hydra—with estimated diameters only between 29 and 106 miles (46 and 170 kilometers).

Watching Charon from Pluto, you would notice something odd. Charon seems to be standing still. Why? Because Pluto's day takes the same amount of time as Charon's orbit around the planet—both just over six days.

Will you find life on Pluto or Charon? No one really knows. After all, no spacecraft has yet visited the planet, and although one is on the way, we won't know a lot about Pluto until it gets there. It's always possible that some form of life— organic or inorganic—exists on this small planet, with some scientists even suggesting that the life forms could be silicate-

like rocks. Or is that just science fiction? When we actually explore Pluto and its moons, we'll know a great deal more.

FINDING PLUTO

A common question on this tour is, "If it's hard to see Pluto even in a telescope on Earth, how did they find it?" The search started in the early 1900s, when astronomers thought there had to be an object pulling on the orbits of Uranus and Neptune. The irregular motions of these planets had to be caused by the gravitational pull of another planet. But even though there were calculations of where the planet should be, it still took more than 30 years to find Pluto. At the Lowell Observatory in Arizona, a young astronomer, Clyde Tombaugh, photographed the tiny object only a short distance from where it was thought to be. In 1930, he discovered the farthest planet in the solar system—Pluto.

We now know that the planet Pluto is too small to have caused Uranus and Neptune to wobble in their orbits. In fact, after calculating the orbits of the two planets more carefully, astronomers realized there really wasn't a wobble. But that "mistake" still led to one of the most astounding discoveries of the twentieth century.

BUT IS PLUTO REALLY A PLANET?

We may talk about Pluto being a planet but not everyone agrees. In fact, scientists are taking a closer look at this tiny member of our solar system and comparing it to some space objects more distant than Pluto. They have discovered many huge objects—some even larger than what we call our "ninth planet"—within the Kuiper Belt, a wide belt of large and small icy bodies just beyond Pluto's orbit. Astronomers believe the bodies are either asteroids, comets, or even burned out comets.

Many of these distant objects are larger than Pluto. For example, scientists discovered Eris in 2003, a space body that measures 1864 miles (3,000 kilometers) in diameter compared to Pluto's 1,467-mile (2,360-kilometer) diameter. Some of these objects have already been named, including Sedna, Orcus, Quaoar, and Eris.

What does this mean? Because of these discoveries, with more found every year, scientists are discussing how to sort out our outer solar system. Will objects over a certain size be called a planet? Will Pluto be stripped of its planetary title and become a dwarf planet or a pluton—names some scientists suggest when talking about the objects? Will we have to welcome more planets to our "member's list" of the solar system? Will some asteroids in the asteroid belt have to be called "planets" because they are bigger, such as the asteroids Vesta, Pallas, and Hygiea? Time will tell before astronomers will settle on what to call these new (and one old—Pluto) members of the outer solar system.

TENTH STOP: BACK TO EARTH

Look back over your shoulder. There, among the stars, you'll see the other members of our solar system. Uranus and Neptune, two tiny blue-green discs, are surrounded by faint rings and many moons. The ringed planet Saturn sits among its many cratered and irregular moons. There is the bright crescent shape of Jupiter, with its many moons circling the planet like a small solar system. And occasionally, we see a flash of sunlight bouncing off an asteroid.

It's time to make your way back toward the inner solar system. As you get closer to the Sun, you'll notice a small blue-white crescent in the sky. This planet is third in line and circles the Sun in about 365 days. It has one large moon. You can see the planet's bright white clouds—and you are no doubt smiling. After visiting all the planets and moons of the solar system, you know that this small planet is the best place for life as we know it to flourish.

Now you realize this planet is just the right distance from the Sun so that it's not too hot or cold. It has great oceans, continents, coral reefs, mountains, river valleys, glaciers, and deserts. It has a perfect balance of air pressure and a combination of gases in its atmosphere that encourages life—from tall and short plants to large and small animals.

Welcome home, space traveler. Welcome back to Earth.

CREDITS

Photos courtesy NASA/JPL/Northwestern University: 9, 12

NASA/JPL-Caltech: 17, 20, 21, 22, 24-25, 28, 30, 35, 40, 42, 52, 53, 54, 56, 71, 73, 74, 75, 76, 77, 79, 81, 82, 85, 93

NASA/NSSDC: 44

NASA/USGS: 31

NASA/JPL/Cornell: 32

ESA/NASA/JPL/University of Arizona: 63

NASA/JPL/Space Science Institute: 50, 59, 61, 62, 66, 67, 68

NASA/JPL/Malin Space Science Systems: 15

NASA/JPL/University of Arizona: 49

NASA/JPL/University of Arizona/University of Colorado: 56

NASA/JPL/ESA/University of Arizona: 64

NASA and the Hubble Heritage Team (STScI/AURA)Acknowledgment: J. Bell (Cornell U.), P. James (U. Toledo), M. Wolff (Space Science Institute), A. Lubenow (STScI), J. Neubert (MIT/Cornell): 27

Alan Stern (Southwest Research Institute), Marc Buie (Lowell Observatory), NASA and ESA: 87

Dr. R. Albrecht, ESA/ESO Space Telescope European Coordinating Facility; NASA: 89

T. Rector (University of Alaska Anchorage), Z. Levay and L. Frattare (Space Telescope Science Institute) and National Optical Astronomy Observatory/Association of Universities for Research in Astronomy/National Science Foundation: 43